Song of My True Self

Song of My True Self

Roberta Lynn Dostal

Published by:
Cawing Crow Press LLC
Dunlo, PA

ISBN: 978-1-68264-006-7

Library of Congress Control Number: 2015955520

Visit us on the web at: www.cawingcrowpress.com

This book is dedicated to
Maureen,
my clinical psychologist
for twenty years
who helped me find
My True Self

Acknowledgements

In 2004 I had to return to Johnstown to care for my aging mother. She was 101 years old and rapidly yielding to the final stages of dementia. Ten months later she passed away.

I had spent three years renovating the home she moved into after my father died in 1972. The house was mine so I decided to stay in Johnstown. I still had a security job to earn extra income in the Exton area where I spent Sundays and Mondays. Twenty-two hours working, eight hours of travel time and three hours sleep in less than thirty-six hours.

I was fortunate when I found a challenge to keep me mentally productive. The University of Pittsburgh at Johnstown has a set-up for senior citizens called, The LearningPLUS Program. If a person is 55 years of age or older and gets the instructor's consent, he or she can take two courses per term-no cost-no credit. Since 2005, I have taken two classes each semester. I can truly say that without becoming involved in the LearningPLUS Program, this book of poetry would not exist.

My first year on campus, I met two of the most dedicated instructors that I ever had through three degrees and three professional licenses.

Dr. Richard Strojan taught me the techniques of writing, especially memoir. I had him for several English classes, but his most significant teaching for me was memoir and autobiography writing. He took the time to evaluate every line of every page when I turned in a seventy-two page final. Even after he retired, he has generously checked each page on two different occasions with the final memoir production being 268 pages. I consider him a special person and a friend.

The first class that I took at UPJ in 2005 was Introduction to Creative Writing taught by Alessandra Lynch. She's still Alessandra Lynch but now the wife of Chris Forhan and the mother of Milo and Oliver Forhan-Lynch. The latter two keep her busy when she isn't teaching in the classroom at Butler University in Indianapolis, Indiana. Alessandra taught me how to put my emotions of both joy and pain into words that the reader related not only with me but also associated with some facet of her or his life. The poems became universal. I am very appreciative of the extra time each week that Professor Lynch donated when reviewing my poetry with me while explaining techniques to improve the structure and composition.

The poetry that she helped me develop was good enough to get me invited to read my works at the 2006 International Conference of the Society for Science, Literature, and the Arts held in Amsterdam.

This book is a tribute to her dedication to the teaching profession.

There are other professors that I've had at UPJ who stimulated interest in both creative nonfiction writing and poetry. A special thanks goes to Michael L. Bodolosky, Dr. Charles Clifton, Dr. Michael Cox, Dr. Jon Darling, Dr. Patty S. Derrick, P K Harmon, Dr. Jeremy C. Justus, Dr. Catharine Kloss, Marissa K. Landrigan, Dr. Cherri Randall, Dr. Eric C. Schwerer, Kevin Stewart, and Dr. Alan Teich.

A note of a special thank you must also be given to the two people who have steered the operations of the LearningPLUS Program since I have been on the UPJ campus. Robert W. Knipple and Jeanne M. Susko always were there for me in registering me into the various classes. Many times they had to work extra hard to keep my computer rights in tack. Most students are gone after four years. I've been hanging around for over ten. When I registered this spring, Bob noted that I'd taken enough courses for two more degrees. The office at the Pitt main campus keeps asking when I am going to graduate.

Aside from faculty members, I must give tribute to a few special staff personnel who helped make my life more pleasant when I was campus: Linda Coyle, secretary in the Humanities Division Department; Patricia Cigich, Janet Grove, and John G. Ziats from the book store; Susan Devan, Robert A. Eckenrod, Craig A. Gresko, Michael Kemock; Ralph M. Miller, Brian L. Moore, Christian J. Phillips, and J Jeffrey Sernell in Information Technology: Technical Services; Andrea Leibfreid and Sharon Wilson of Social Science Division; Frank L. Dupnock and Paulette Lewis at the post office; Daniel Gotwald in the print shop; Joan Keirn in the Learning Lab; and George A. Hancock in the Registrar's Office.

One cannot be on campus without offering their gratitude to the members of the Police Department and the Maintenance Plant. There are too many names to mention everyone in these areas, but I can't leave without mentioning Gloria Lehman. I would tease her when I saw her communicating with another person by singing the following verse, "Gloria, Gloria, praise be to God there are no more of you."

I am also grateful to all of the students who critiqued my papers in the different classes. Many of their suggestions offered new pathways in my thinking of presenting my works.

I also need to give kind words to my editor Craig Grossman of Cawing Crow Press LLC whose suggestions and editing helped improve dynamics of this publication.

Most of all, I have to thank Dr. Maureen Lynn Osborne to who this poetry book is dedicated. Maureen was my therapist for twenty years. She guided me through eliminating many of the negative personality traits that resulted from being abused by a Catholic priest prior to adulthood. She served as my advisor and mentor as I transitioned from the male world to female gender that had haunted me from my early days as a child. She became my surrogate mother to help my inner child Cameli and I grow as the result of neglect of motherly attention in childhood.

Maureen helped ease the pain of a divorce after 51 years of marriage. Now she's gone-retired, but will always remain part of my character. Needless to say, there have been tears shed in attempting to loosen the bonds of attachment that I have for this woman. However, I planted the seeds in her mind of me, much as Pavlov did with the dogs, so when she sees a humming bird, she will think of me. Thank you Maureen for everything that you did for me.

It is difficult to name everyone who has been kind and helpful to me since my transition but several persons need recognized: Jeanne Dostal, my three sons: James, Joseph, and especially Jason; Alan and Cheryl Pittenger; Attorney Richard M. Serbin; Mary Ann Ruscio; Casey Gilmore Aspin and David Aspin; Dr. Nancy Chiswick; Dr. Rosemarie Leuzzi; Cooper University Physican, Voorhees, New Jersey; Dr. Elihu Goren; Mary Lodge; Friends from the Main Line Unitarian Church, especially Vincent Craig, Jessica Hirsch Lynn, Jan Cauffman, and Rev. Morgan McLean; Unitarian Congregation of West Chester; Employees at Value-it in Johnstown, especially Ken, Brad, and Wendy; Amir Hassain; Lee Barrett from Lancaster Theological Seminary; and my friendly neighbors in BonAir that is a community in Johnstown, Pennsylvania.

Introduction

My intent in publishing this book of poetry is to record a journey of my life. Many stages have come and gone, but each has left memories of the positive and the negative events that occurred. During my life I have met many people who would leave a distinct impression with me. Some I've tried hard to forget while others I hold like a valuable gold coin-one that I would never want to lose or have taken away from me. I have experienced many events that were sorrowful, painful, and depressing. Other times, joyful, pleasurable, and memorable activities lifted my spirits to a level of extreme happiness. However, like most people, my days were filled with emotions related to the issues confounding me. While the words in my poems are about my life, I hope that they can find a ground that speaks to your feelings. I am not the only child neglected in childhood. I am not the only person sexually abused by a Catholic priest. I am not the only individual who suffered a gender identity crisis. I am not the only adult divorced by their mate. I am not the only human being to lose the person who I felt was irreplaceable. The world is overflowing with people who have had or are having the same or similar dilemmas.

In the poems of my childhood, I hope that we can hold hands. During adolescence, you might feel the same frustrations and hardships. As I offer a moment of maturity, you can say, "I've been there." We all have families that can be helpful or thorns in our saddle as we attempt to circumvent difficult problems or maybe you can smile and say, "Yes, we did that every Christmas." We all have passions that set goals within our expectations. Often we may be disappointed, other times maybe even envious of another's achievements, or occasionally, we are the winners on top of the heap. It is my wish that you can understand my loneliness. Can you feel the anxiety on being penetrated by a Catholic priest prior to puberty? Feel the confusion of doubt that plagued my identity. Understand my acceptance of a divorce. If you are old, let's walk the road together. If you are not, think of me when you get there.

Come walk with me through the lines of my poetry. Let my words be your thoughts. Find beauty in the sharing of myself with you.

The arrangement of the poetry in this book is meant to follow a loose pattern that reflects the various periods of my life. I will start with works that bring highlights of my early childhood and grade school period that will be viewed in Khaki Kangaroo, Swimming Holes, and My Home Town.

During adolescence, please feel the pain and suffering I experienced when sexually abused by Catholic priest over a two year period when you read Phantom Man. The sterile attitude and response by the church hierarchy when I disclosed the action of this priest fifty years later was even worse. Crucifixion speaks to this statement.

My life took a turn for the better when I attended Don Bosco Agricultural High School in Huttonsville, West Virginia. Rejoice in my growth as you read Farmall H, and Tombstone. Be amused by First Experience.

During the previous two periods of my life, my family needs to be mentioned. Happy Birthday Son, Father and Mother tell you how I felt.

My education advanced when I graduated from Pennsylvania State University and began a teaching career. Follow my progress as I venture on into learning when you read Enlightenment. Time spent in daily activities, marriage, parenting were the activities for the next thirty years that offered many opportunities for growth, learning, enjoyment, and disappointments. Who Am I, Expectations, and Good-bye Robert speak to this period. My inner voice with a mental image of a young girl, which would eventually be known as Cameli, let me realize my true identity as a human being.

I took a sabbatical in 1976 to study horticulture at Penn State. It was there that I first received the benefits of entering the world of psychology. Dr. Nancy Chriswick introduced me to myself. I now clearly realized my need to change genders. However, I also know that that if I had completed the transition in 1977, I would have been fired from my public high school teaching position. I had a wife and three children to support, so I waited. *Bobbi's Voyage* was one of the first poems that I wrote about my struggle.

I transitioned in 1996 and completed the physical aspects of becoming a woman on June 8, 1999 in Montreal, Canada. It was ironic that I would return to the city that had been a place of hatred for so many years. Montreal was one of the areas that the pedophilia. Fr. Mario R. Fabbri, had taken me as a youth to perform his acts of sexual abuse. Fortunately, it would be one of the locations outside of the United States that would change my status on the stature of limitation on his activities. I mention these points of history as they influenced my emotional thinking in the poetry that I've written.

Bottled Message explains the results of my desire to become a chaplain in the Unitarian-Universalist when attending a Christian seminary after having surgery. The period after attending the seminary was an extremely lonely phase of my life. *Christmas Wreath, Pink Slippers*, and *Sylvia's Path* are associated with this period. Poetry dealing with my mother, siblings, and immediate family included such works as *Killer, Colors. Crystals* and *Little Creek.*

I returned to my native community of Johnstown in 2004 to assist my aging mother. My attendance at the University of Pittsburgh at Johnstown launched my writing career and my love of poetry. It helped me express my feelings. I have spent the last ten years taking mostly writing and literature courses at the above university. The majority of my poetry was composed as the result of doing assignments for course work at UPJ. *Geologic Vegetable Beef Stew* was one of the first poems that I wrote on campus. Many more would follow thanks to instructors like Alessandra Lynch.

I have also taken the time to attend many of the summer writing programs offered by various universities on the northeastern part of United States. Poems such as *Old Upright, Nothing Poem, Quiet Time, Who Am I,* and *Sonnet of Simplicity* were crystalized during attendance at these functions.

After 20 years of being my beacon of light as a mentor, therapist, and surrogate mother, Dr. Maureen Osborne retired as a psychotherapist. Lament of *Surrogate Mother, Broken Barriers, Lament on a Premature Termination,* and *Happy Daughter Poem* are tributes of my thankfulness of having her as a therapist.

There a number of poems that offer a portrait of me such as *Time Shift*, *One Act Play,* and *Getting Old.* The final poem, the one that tells the best story of me, is *A Song of My True Self.*

—Roberta Lynn Dostal, 2015

Contents

Childhood

Khaki Kangaroo

Mom saved your tattered khaki hide,
storing you in a cardboard box,
along with other childhood toys
I proudly call my own today,
but don't recall you as one.
You were held tightly in my arms,
or hurled from my wooden crib,
but sometimes resting all alone.
I would bet that I peed on you,
and maybe some days even worse.

Aged cloth now forms your outlined frame,
still dirty and worn from child wear,
faded color stuffed with something,
legs need mended to make you whole,
your age numbers my golden years.
I often speculate why you
were not a fluffy teddy bear.
Might it be I was different then,
wanting to explore many things,
so they gave me a kangaroo.

Enclosed in glass but not a tomb,
I have you displayed on a shelf
among items I call treasures.
I wish my mind could recreate,
the love I must have had for you.

My Home Town

The sky seesawed between a grayish white and reddish orange,

I only learned on summer vacation that the sky might really be blue. The

soil of the back yard couldn't support any real green grass,

only the hardiness of perennial flowers plus weeds could grow.

Cars and houses and everything were covered with a reddish dust,

rain helped wash it away with the mine drainage to the orange river.

Every night the mills generated two sparkling bright fireworks,

loading the molten slag came first followed by the dumping in Park Hill.

Anyone who wanted to sacrifice his body for a buck could get a job,

all you needed was desire, spirit, and maybe a pair of good gloves.

Three times a day brave men crossed the bridge from my hometown,

hundreds marched with a full pail of food plus their favorite legal drink.

They came back slower, tired, weary, dirty, and maybe bruised.

many stopped along the way for a cold glass or two of liquid empathy.

The same routine was followed by those working on the railroads,

and black faces emerged from the cold, dusty, and dangerous mines.
The reward of a paycheck grew with each year of service,
the war had pushed industry to its peak of production.

Taxes in the borough from the property where the steel was made,
made this small hillside of Franklin the richest in the entire state.
The U S of A grew with steel, coal, and transportation as the stars,
this fantasy world of employment happily danced on the union's stage.
Rocket sixty years ahead and stand on the same street bricks of my home town,
gone is each star, the march, the smoke, the sparks, the buckets, and bars.
The young ones look confused when you mention the word, roundhouse,
how can they know any better as all the tracks and trains are gone?
The mines are now manned by ghosts and in memories of past workers,
visit the tourist mine attraction that helps keep the wounded city alive.
Come and see the flood museum and the huge hole where it all started,
the Incline Plane, but hurry if you want to see the Bandstand in Roxbury Park.

Learning Revenge

The faint glow of a corner streetlight
illuminated the deserted alley
of dirt as scratchy sounds vibrated
from feet scraping steps toward home--
steel mill dirt, my feet, my home.
No ghosts or goblins stirred in my mind,
only the image of a man's grouchy face:
unshaven, toothless, and beady eyed
below a bald surface with scowling sounds
voiced toward passing kids like me.
His unpainted house, weathered boards,
bowed roof, and sagging porch
while surrounded by aged wooden fence,
painting a dying mental canvas as
a shadow followed my charted trail.
That biting cold October night,
Halloween was still in the future
but here my body stopped,

looking at the decaying fence,
a symbol to a time long past.

Moist and mossy slats, the heads
of rusted nails gone, the wind brings
the lines of standing wood to life.
Revenge of his mean voice finds life
by the silence from his darkened house.
One board, then two, it was so easy
for a ten year old to do.
The crack was quiet, barely heard,
as the push against a post dominoed
all the slats toward a waiting earth.

The evidence of green slime,
a visible memory from my past,
sticks to faded dungarees where hands
wiped the evidence of guilt and shame
from a deed committed out of spite.

Peace of Nun

Tall, black, terrorizing—haloed in white,
beads, strong enough to strangle,
straddled the side—a cross to remind one
of the consequences of failure. Piercing eyes
framed in spectacles on a crooked nose,
radiate a glare—draining guilt and shame
from the soul. A smile would crack that porcelain
face. Deep furrows plowed in a forehead
from years of frowning, cast shadows--grave
mounds to come. Notches in a ruler—
evidence of blood drawing on victim's
sore knuckles. A voice, not feminine,
lacking compassion and understanding.
Children follow like ducklings, like pets
in the shadow of this surrogate parent.
Memories, memories—bad memories—
buried in the terrible years of torment.
Drop a twenty on the store counter, clinch
the doll replica, exit, and smash it against the wall.

Street Car

Steel tracks, steel wheels, brick streets,
steel car, steel doors, wooden seats,
transportation of my youth still remembered.

Steel cable touching hot steel wire,
surging source of electrical power,
transporting a safe, orange, steel box.

Wires cobweb the tinted steel town sky
at intersections. Why did the orange spiders die—
were they part of the steel mill equation?

The end of line is the beginning of another,
raise the front pole, drop the back,
transfer collection box from back to front.

Enjoy a brief rest, check forgotten items,
fill empty slots in metal belt coin dispenser,
backtrack to the original destination.

A plain male uniformed in dark blue,
or was it black, the color of his special hat,
transformed the man into a conductor.

Each day ended sending the trolley to the car barn,
to be cleaned and put to rest for another night,
transition from wear and tear to idleness.

Would a child's desire to be conductor die,
like the street car on steel rails,
transferring changing images of life?

Swimming Holes

’40’s sunshine, tanning eager youngsters
thirsting to dip and dunk in cool water,
glistened on roads to swimming hole destinations.

Public pools was attended by youth who hadn’t
squandered allowances or had baby-sitting quarters.
There were days when I swam alone

The first only required a walk across the Franklin Bridge
from East Conemaugh to catch the downtown streetcar,
transfer, on to Bens Creek, and a remaining half-mile
hike to Ideal Park’s fifty cents admission open-air
pool. Buoyed bodies in water that once cast shadows
on the concrete bottom are now memories in minds.

Twenty-five cents admitted a person to Liberty Park but
the six-mile walk toward South Fork discouraged many.
The walls holding water have now crumbled having surrendered
to community pools and back-yards with blue rubber liners.

A two-mile walk from Conemaugh to Echo and then
getting down the steep hill where the woods
opened into the Little Conemaugh River was free
The water sparkled with yellow mine drainage
but that wasn’t any worse than the water at Liberty
and Ideal where lazy swimmers just peed in the water.

The small creek where crabs scooted faster than our fingers
moved meandered up the hill above East Conemaugh.
Shovels of mud, stones, and soggy leaves filled the brown
pores of burlap potato bags secured from Weavers,
a grocery store on Main Street. When the stream
was damned, we skinny-dipped in the dark.
The only the light came from burning limbs surrounded
by sandstone rocks that sent burst of sizzling pieces onto
dry clothes that developed holes mothers questioned.

Winter waters cut the breast of the decaying cloth-soaked sacks
but left no scars in my memory of a private swimming hole.

Impression

Not even stirring the dusty hollyhocks on either side
of the dirt alley, an old horse, its head hung low,
its back bowed, belly ribs showing, a clip-clopping sound
as it hoofs up mother earth, leaving only the sign of luck.

A lazy-moving worn wooden wagon filled with nothing
follows, its turning wooden spoke wheels squeaking
a low answer to the tired horse pulling in front.

Perched atop the rigging, on a flat board with a rug cushion,
sits a tired looking old dark skinned man, sad eyes,
almost asleep, white wiry hair haloing a sweaty brow,
body carrying the same bent frame as the horse,
the reins in his weary hands hang and sway loosely.

A mental photograph hung fifty-five years ago in my youth.

Adolescence

Phantom Man

Thick lens over slick eyes--Gray circling a black dot center.
Sly tinted glasses send his stalking stare into obscurity.

A receding hair line follows the pattern of an eroding New England shoreline,
light glistens off a bare beach, a whitish straw plastered in water and oil.

His illness hidden behind a pure white round collar and a jet black suit,
his mind short circuits affections for God and young boys.

No fox or wolf more cunning in luring and stalking an innocent lamb.
The pedophile's net of security covers all suspicions of wrongful detection.

Parents are unsuspecting providers in their zeal to see their child flourish.
What better environment than to be in the hands of a guiding priest.

The hinges of the trap are constructed of religious training: the man is holy.
The cheese bait varies from spiritual, to mental, to a materialistic nature.

Once the spring has sprung and the innocent has fallen into the snare of doubt,
the abuser tangles and twist the ropes of the deceived's will in doubtful knots.

The abused, chained to silence by fear of omission, is secured with the lock of guilt,
while the man of the cloth defies the sanctuary of human dignity.

Time can end the relation but never cure to spiritual damage of lost innocence,
the victim's growth stagnates into maturity in a totally unusual dimension.

Dealing with a tarnished religious past depends upon each person's inner strength,
suicide is the worst, substances bury many, but a few claim to be survivors.

Those who made it through the gauntlet of religious confusion and self-forgiveness,
are challenged by mocking pillars of faith that need to be smashed to the ground.

Bishops become horses with blinders focused only on saving a diminishing faith,
unidentified molesters skillfully move to protect the image of their unstained purity.

Accusers are tainted. No loving hand is offered healing and understanding,
their allegations rise like balloons targeted in the sights of guided enemy arrows.

Struggles continue in the ranks of learned appointed church officials who cried,
"Bury this disease quickly and make smooth the way for our lacking followers."

Those who understand the message left by the Man who was nailed to a cross,
know it wasn't the same dogma being proclaimed by the man with the golden staff.

First Experience

Flesh, real flesh,
skin, real skin,
the female beacon,
majestic teat,
the young look,
the mature play,
the old dream,
death buries life.
I read the poem,
I am twelve.
I look old for my age,
next year an adolescent.
I want to know things,
things that make learning fun.
Hard, it is hard,
I feel the urge.
Take it slowly,
move with caution.
Her eyes stare as if I'm intruding,
I want to try it, just once.
Her reddish chestnut hair,
reflects the light of learning.
My hand touches the surface,
it is warm, truly inviting.
I squeeze, she doesn't flinch, I rub,
she is responding.
Her body isn't tense,
she flows between the legs.

I bend and lick with pleasure,
the sweet cream of life.
I straighten to catch my breath
I am here, it is now.

A new experience,
a star in an age of innocence, I am
complete for the moment,
I just milked a Jersey cow.

Tombstone

Resting as a testament for their foundation,

one single building isn't inscribed with names.

How many ghosts still linger in memory,

capturing the images of a lonely past.

Boys struggling to become men,

male guidance without female aprons.

Days busy, activities changing by hour,

chores, games, classes, church, and dishes.

Nights alone and long, dreams offering pleasure,

sunlight, cows and manure greeting the morning.

The school is gone, the priests are dead,

the ghosts living to tell their tale.

Success stories of survival in youth,

few visible scars but others buried deep.

Individuals becoming solid bricks for the future,

yielding now to those who follow.

The already crumbled are fondly remembered,

along with the ghosts who dance here today.

We live the vision of a core transplanted

on a valley farm in West Virginia mountains.

Farmall H

On the farm, she did it all,
that's how they named her.
Now her body shows signs of aging
with tires of hard cracked rubber.

She doesn't start as quickly
as when her first battery sparked.
She can't move as gracefully
as when her bearings were new.

Her skin of red and white has faded,
tinted slightly gray by sun's rays.
While dumping the digested food returned,
she stalls or sputters with the load.

Her dim lights from frosted glass
make the furrows hard to find.
Her days and events are numbered.
Young ones drift toward newer models.

Yet here she stands in glory,
over accomplished feats of wonder.
Can any more or less be said
of the boys who once drove her?

Family

Happy Birthday Son

I believe you're 47,

you are special.

My, how time flies,

I'm 72,

When I was 47,

you were 25.

When I was 25,

my Dad was 62.

When you are 62,

Dad and I are done.

Happy Birthday Son,

Outcome

At the fork in the road,

the decision was made.

Was the turn right,

should it have been left?

The change selected

wasn't a real choice.

Simply the only direction

to eliminate the infection.

Sun's rays now greet the day,

but the night has a new moon.

Unheard voices of yesterday

bred unexpected losses.

She really didn't understand

my collar of daily dilemma--

betrayal her imaged answer,
Isolation her chosen solution.
Three creations visible,
the first stands last,
the middle still middle.
the last placing first.
Time died of aging cancer,
voiding its cliche of healing.
Cure is masked in solitude
seeking help from hidden hands.
Gems of freedom glow,
knowledge the only gold,
Silver the lesser metal,
spirit revealed in music.
I have my earned treasure
In a large empty container,
locked by my nothingness
and sealed with loneliness.

Ears channel echoes

to a weak eroding heart.

Words pulsate vibrations of life.

Speak gentle voice of wisdom.

Father

I never called you, "Daddy,"

just "Pop."

Who let it happen?

Was it written in stone in your heart?

I loved you,

admired your work,

was proud of you,

you spoke seven languages,

you were a real doctor.

I needed to be with you,

but you were distant.

Was it rejection or simply not knowing?

Did we share haunting memories of loneliness?

Was it because I was your fourth?

Were material things expressions of your love?

You are gone,

the answers are buried.

My children know you,

you taught me your way--

they now wonder if I care.

I ask you Daddy,

I wish you could respond,

“Did your soul ever beg

with your heart crying

for your father to say,

‘ Son, I love you!

How are you today?’ ”

Time Keeper

Red images break the dark,

numbers radiating from a clock

suspended in the night,

offer comfort to eyes

while I wait to enter

an unknown journey.

11:29 -- November twenty-ninth,

the month and day cradles my birth.

Time passes between red changes.

11: 34 -- The month and year holds my birth,

11:58 -- still awake on our wedding date.

11:59 – She's pregnant.

Years disappear after 12:59

until the 1:00,

a new and different century.

But months and days

still appear in the night,

1:20 -- January 20

number one son arrives,

followed by #2 at 5:30

and #3 on 8:26.

Change splits the bond of love.

6:08 occurs with 6:99 an illusion,

but neither are accepted.

Red ticks towards morning.

I watch time repeat my living days,

wondering off a fading stage

and a dream yet to come.

Tiny Critters

Leave that ant hill to grow in green, grassy lawn,

To someday stand out like an oasis in the desert.

The tiny black clusters of beaded bodies dart,

from nowhere and return there.

The pattern of their highways is like

driving a tractor-trailer through the Bronx.

How many tunnels have these eager eaters mined under your lawn,

you could get a shovel if you really thought it was important.

Is something more destructive occurring below the ground,

or are they harmless little pests when viewing the big picture?

How do these tiny critters determine whose property to invade?

Is my land prime real estate due to my beautiful peonies?

Nature seeks a place like a lovely flower,

big and small, short and tall.

Elizabeth Belle, my sister, had two beautiful breast at her peak,

that disappeared when cancer cells ate her away to death.

Military Service

He took the bullet for his blunder.
No, he wasn't snipered dead,
but he easily could have been.
At forty-six, my father was old,
but still enlisted in the army.
Medical doctors were in demand.
His tour of duty was lengthy,
covered all of World War II,
and stationed on foreign soils.
Censored notes from Australia, tribal
trinkets came from the medicine man,
but never a word when in New Guinea.
He was somewhere gone;
I was too small to understand,
but knew I missed my father.
He didn't have to go to war,
not a choice given youthful men;

he needed this space for an ending.
His was a decision to end an affair,
one that cut deep into mother's heart,
leaving scars with her that inflicted me.

He returned after the mushroom cloud,
a different person than the father
who left me when I was only eight.

He died a natural death decades later,
never telling me why he'd gone,
but an older voice narrated his reason.
His time in the military service,
designed to mend a failing marriage,
left one flag to salute—the purity of honor.

The Look

I know her look. I see her look
of excitement through forty years.
The look appearing on her face,
still a face without aging lines
after seven decades and counting.

A face that won a college pageant
now views the unopened package,
the children's books,
the pictures of my parents, and
trinkets treasured by my mother.

A child-like look of pleasure,
waltzing through years two to ten in a peaceful trance,
her orange crate dollhouse, paper dolls, imagined
children, moving forward in time, a moment
with someone else, or a good day with me.

The look ends, leaving a void gaze,
a period of silence as the faucet drips.
Another look stirs, confused,
a look of lost time, our time,
a look with a different message.
I am the she that she
doesn't want me to be.
But here I am, watching these looks,
my mind twisting and turning,
knowing the looks can't alter tomorrow.

Tonight I will return, to my space, a different dwelling,
another departure clothed in darkness.
She'll remain, closing her storybook again,
but wondering how her golden years
were lost when she was always looking.

Mother

I hold her hand, gently
caressing each finger, softly
stroking the skin, loosely
hanging on fragile bone.

Her eyes close, slowly
the bell sounds, quietly
posting the hour, tenderly
announcing the need ahead.

I watch her breathe, silently
noting the movement, carefully
sensing the struggle, calmly
praying for the painless end.

The wind outside stirs, gracefully

lifting dry leaves, delicately

rustling nature, peacefully

placing mother in His arms.

Photograph

Black over white—a silhouette,
image of her past—a memory.
Crowned beauty—long ago--college,
now a closed beauty school logo.
Clouds of misfortune pave her way,
mobility slowed but not intellect.
Chance or fate—God won't tell,
her loves die or change.
Children come, grandkids follow,
a family tree slowly growing.
I am there but am not,
it's uncertain if I was ever.
Her pain and joy interchange
with my moods and dilemmas.
I'm to blame for her sorrow,
my excuse yet to be determined.
Our inner selves have shifted,
we share separate spaces.
Once dependent, she thrives alone,
I am different, simple opposite.
Golden years are mists,

thoughts of lost tomorrows.

Today living, yesterday a past,

Tomorrow, a picture fading.

Another Fall

Is it the loss of a summer season full of freedom in your presence?

Do the dark clouds hanging in the sky signal drowning waves of remorse?

We are in different galaxies without you here holding a hand beside me.

Your space was part of my loving circle but now has changed positions.

Frosty white homes appear as shadows of emptiness and loneliness.

No cheers from a joyous stadium uplift my sadden heart as I stroll.

The shining sun fails to ignite my spirit of joy or brighten my gloomy day.

Your absence leaves a void of excitement that once inhabited my body.

The environment surrounding me does not seem to understand the pain.

hurt where no one can feel, see, or touch my soul of inner sorrows.

I reach back to a shadow of our past only to be denied consoling entry.

I need the surviving secret to the misery when two hearts are cut apart.

Your simple ways of sharing and offering me avenues to your heart,
now echo tunes from tight strings and other games you helped me play.
Nights are struggles with sleep and dreams that can't bury your memory.
Your tender voice of innocence keeps circling in my mind each minute.

Oh, you swirling leaves that wisp between my feet, head, and the ground.
Become alive with the love by a special force to aid in my desired comfort.
Camouflage my choices of decisions in a curtain of dancing fall colors,
let me walk among you without regret for a self-inflicted broken heart.

Little Girl

Conceived not in my womb, tender
umbilical cord of her mind attaches
to me professionally.
The child nurses breasts of empathy,
cuddles arms of acceptance,
grasps my little finger for security.
Eyes dancing with first steps--
arms reaching, renewing support.
Face smiling in toddling efforts,
fear, pain, tears with each fall.
I mother her toward adolescence.
She believes in Santa Claus,
the tooth fairy, and certain people—
all balloons popping with rejection
as the journey of growth continues—
desires love but is a loner.
Clear minded in survival techniques,
lost in shadows with self acceptance,
she struggles with ideology awarding
the crown of emotional affection to
physical dilemma over mental anguish.

She wades uncertain at water's edge--

a mother's reach is limited.

Will she remember how to swim?

Does she desire the opposite shore?

Your Dream, My World

Symbolism of life,

half the boiled egg before us,

contrasts the remainder of the next life--

hidden.

Only the white,

representing the pure and holy

aspects of my father's life,

is present.

The hollow center,

filled with his charity

to humankind as a physician,

is overflowing.

The yoke,

discolored

and discarded from this altar,

signifies his earthly faults,

forgiven and forgotten.

I,

his unknown daughter,

goddess of transwomen,

weep his loss.

Slowly,

placing the gift of protein in sealed glass,

deposit the vessel

in my silk-lined pocket.

The act,

metaphorizes the sperms

he cast into the belly

of my fertile mother,

producing my birth.

Here,

before the wall of goddesses,

I assign him

the most fitting for his eternity.

Eostre,

goddess of the resurrection of life--

the egg,

her symbol for eternal remembrance.

Prior to Surgery

Enlightenment

As an Earth Science major in geology
my field touched the heart of Mother Earth.
Fallen angels still struggled for power
as one combed the deserts and mountains.
Wassach offered beauty with the hidden beasts,
as dusty trails choked a dry mouth.
Sun god beat and charred the skin,
sucking oils for the next day's fire.
Eyes pelleted with sand by god of wind,
sweat crystallizing as salt to lick for health.
Paradise was cleansing these ungodly acts
in a stream fed by mountain waters.

Who Am I

Do I need a song to sing,

to let an ear hear my praise?

Notes with words about my past,

citing the degrees achieved.

Who would be interested?

My resume divulges graduation

from grade and high school,

bachelors from a university,

and three masters add dignity.

But all made of paper.

Only two jobs to gain retirement,

a teacher of children,

minds on prime time

offered secondary education.

I think I gave them more.

Three professional licenses

helped me earn extra money,

served as an influences to each child,

each choosing one for their career.

Should I have been a doctor?

I can cook, craft a desk of wood,

paint a picture, grade a quarter,

appraise a vase, sell a store,

produce peppers, and identify a stone.

Maybe write a poem?

I've had a lot of appealing hobbies,

earned a living in special ways,

I kept growing, but what catches my eye

as I yield to the years, empty spaces,

the dealings that I didn't do.

Expectations

It is the lonely times,

the nights offering no fulfillment

that stir an emotional storm.

Loneliness isn’t a welcomed friend but an enemy

whose visits can assassinate the desire to live.

A career of glory ended with shattered bones shattering

the celebrity images of personal fame.

Previous success and recognition molded

elevated expectations initiating
a void that when the body broke,
the loneliness led to a lead bullet exploding

and exploring his lonely mind.

Was it duck, goose, or synthetic stuffing
that muffled the thunder?
The sound left no echo in a despondent brain

as the metal passed as quickly as the thought

from the mind to press the trigger.

The NFL channel still booming in the background.

Who creates these expectations of grandeur?

Who’s to blame?

Is anyone to blame?

Someone must be blamed.

Think about the dilemma of expectations.
What releases the latch of *Pandora's Box*
Rejection and failure seem to be the grim keys
that allow the monster of depression to emerge.

What makes a stable person unstable?
Is being too independent,
rarely requesting assistance,
the springboard to rejection?

Is the need to ask for help, that a person can't request,
an admission of failure that torments the disposition into depression?
If let down, does the trap door to anguish release,
allowing a person to fall into despair?

Is success in intimacy stymied by a personality can lead to isolation—
the foundation of mental instability? Didn't he have a friend to call?

Dark clouds may hover on a horizon.
Are they clouds from verbal abuse,
parents pushing,
wanting success for a child
where the adults failed?

Is it striving for the unobtainable perfection?

Has our society set the stakes too high and created constant stress?

Someone is responsible for generating illusory goals.

Who is it:

coaches
with the need to win at any cost,
teachers
without compassion for students' ability,
students
with self-centered personalities,
religions
without a conscience for truth,
corporate executives
with only a drive for personal wealth,
politicians
without morals,
lawyers
with principles built on greed,
you and I
without awareness for another's needs?

Empathy, Empathy,
both for the victim,
and for those left behind.

Good-bye Robert

Every second of every minute, hour, day, week, month, and year
you were my life. You held me in bondage with mental straps
that violated my identity. However, I escaped.

You were the individual who cast clouds of doubt in our mind
through our shared body and associations. Your way
left my spouse and children with memories and impressions
that now stigmatize me and cause them pain.

I will amend your careless remarks, your self-centered activities,
your lack of affection, your doubts of trust, your anger,
and your lack of patience. Oh, I understand your frustrations.

You have just cause to claim support for your actions
based on circumstances. Fortunately, those days are gone forever
and I grant you amnesty. However, this is the here and now.

You were the person I was supposed to be that nature spoiled.
I am now in control. I will not harm those who need healing, suffer
losses, long for kind words and seek attention.

I will not attempt to buy their love with gifts that only gather dust,
nor will I feed on the misconception that they are indebted to me for
the years of my caring for their financial requirements.

I will build an image as the understanding person I feel that I am for both
of our benefits. I will be patient. I will wait for my family to recognize
the difference between you and me without forcing the issue in
a controlling manner as you might have done.

I will wait for each of them to find me through their own form of love
and acceptance. While I wait, I will welcome myself to your fading
world, for I am the special person that you should have been.

Robert,

I said good-bye to you the night before surgery on June 8 of 1999.
Since then, your memory lurks in and out of the shadows of my daily
life. My mother grasped to the illusive hope that I was merely a
stage you needed to resolve. Jeanne lived with you in
the past and mourns your parting, but she knows me.

The time has come that I must softly whisper final good-byes to you.
You as me will no longer ever be.
Good-bye Robert.

Bobbi's Voyage

Upon the vast ocean of silent living,

I sail in an obscure tiny but fragile boat.

Pondering an uncharted course with some misgiving,

I feel terribly alone and so very remote.

Most days the wind and rain violently blow,

yet there are times when the sun seems to shine.

But alias the drifting mind always comes to know,

that society mans the helm and keeps the waves in line.

There must be ways that surely have some bearing,

as I look to the guiding beacon light for assistance.

And seek friends and relations, who might be caring,

only to find they are all lost in their own existence.

There are no demons controlling or pulling me down,

nor any angels with miracles to complete my desire.

Just delightful thoughts and wishes that swirl around,

seeking a female body to anchor a normal attire.

A strong course of action now enters my mind,

    row forward not turning back to see where I've been.

I look for the island where people would be kind,

    and allow me to be whole while emerging from him.

However, reality sinks in with a shivery chill,

    the many efforts have produced no motion.

My progress has really remained quite still,

    as I realize my dream was just a fruitless notion.

And now I look to myself with certain blame,

    and yield to the forces that harbor within me.

Thus letting the anger, hate, guilt and shame,

    smash my vessel of hope in a drowning sea.

After Surgery

Bottled Message

Red sandstone buildings touched deep nostalgia into the past.
An origin unidentified-- travels through the westernwilderness,
another college setting, the simple color of youthful mill pollution,
or the layers of nature's formations stamped the site with approval.
Couple the feeling with coming intentions, the campus served as the
foundation to complete the task of becoming a Unitarian minister.
Two years later, the dream, evolving into a nightmare, ended.
Awakened by the reality that conflicting views with professors and
district evaluators established who was in authority. Being female of a
different nature with a voice not afraid to express opinions didn't help
build confidence with supporters for ordination. Evidence of the ability
to communicate with the suffering were never considered. Doubts of
Jesus as God closed the gates to the seminary while too deep a
spirituality drowned denomination acceptance. It was over!
Fading are the memories of spiritual experiences in the historic chapel.
Fading are thoughts exchanged with teachers and fellow students.
Friendships that were bonded in feelings of intimacy are slipping from
closeness. What hasn't faded are the old and sick people in homes
and hospitals whose eyes said thank you for their spiritual comfort.

Clock Movements

His weak legs needed to rock forward
and backward to stand, like a pendulum
swinging and recording time until
his naked body fell as legs slid
between the toilet, his head rang
as it struck the shower floor,
his medical alarm hanging on the doorknob,
out of reach. Before a neighbor found him
his clocks had ticked away for half-a-day.
Now he rocks back and forth in a nursing home.
Two months after his accident, I purchased
his furniture, appliances, and clocks.
I arranged to bring him home for a last visit
before removing merchandise from the house.
He was shaky as we ascended the steep driveway.
In each of the six rooms, he picked through the dust,
case knife hidden in the rare chestnut roll top desk,
Playboy magazines stored under the bed,
miniature china pitchers arranged on the wall shelves,
a Mother-of-Pearl case with an ivory face in the bedroom,
black and white photographs of a youngster in mother's arms,
but quickly stuck a letter in his pocket—sacred.
Most of all, we talked about clocks.
Every room adorned with evidence of his special talent.
Clocks and fifty years of trade magazines,
books on clock history and repair,

gears, springs, shafts, two dozen rusty
c-clamps, twenty shiny tweezers,
and a six-foot grandfather clock
without any heart waiting for a donor.
My living room is now filled with clocks and
a hundred boxes of brass, steel, and wooden
gears. Hands, weights, and keys fill my cellar.
During the month of packing his clocks,
I slept in his bed, cooked on his stove, and sat in his chair,
I went to dinner with the neighbor who rescued him
and visited the old gentleman at the nursing home.
I still live alone with my bad knees and hips.
I don't even have an emergency beeper.
My two-story home also has six rooms
Filled with my treasures: 1939 World's Fair tram car
and trailer, Native American turquoise jewelry,
fifteen years of weekly recorded cassettes
and tapes of personal history, and now twenty-three
antique clocks ticking and sounding their chimes.
I haven't yet reached the need to rock to stand,
but I look at each clock contemplating
the reminder of its allotted time?

Crucifixion

Years have passed and now the sad story can be told,
time has taken me from a youth to being old.
The priest was granted trust in guidance to be used,
which ended in my being sexually abused.
This innocent child was to suffer terrible shame,
and led to believe that I was also to blame.
No millstone and trip for the priest to the sea,
the Church simply let the pedophile be.
Thoughts of the bodily pain only surface at my will,
but the mental damage of loss and hurt lingers still. Another
good person suffered a great deal of pain,
which is used to influence a mind that is sane.
His name was Jesus and on a cross he once died,
the world believed, and for Him, they prayed and cried.
His actions were to save the sinners on this earth,
his teachings do help one reach a much higher berth.
"Be thankful the Man doesn't have to go to court today," I shout,
for his statute of limitations would have run out.

Killer

I ended your marriage,
    I killed your husband,
        I found freedom.
I hurt the children,
    I killed their father.
        I found freedom.
I caused a mother pain,
    I killed her son,
        I found freedom.
I shocked siblings
    I killed their brother
        I found freedom.
I destroyed the family,
    I killed myself,
        I found freedom.
I had surgery,
    I became a woman
        I found freedom.

Colors

Pink lady, blue boy, gays celebrate rainbows--
earth's blend of light, lesbian purple,
sun and rain combine
producing spectrum colors.
God's pictured white, Virgin could be black,
angels in golden halos,
devils grow red tails with sharp spikes.
Irish love green, Scot's orange,
provide battle color conflicts.
African-American's black,
Native-American's red.
America: red, white, and blue,
all glow in vibrant images.
Orange caution, red stop,
Yellow tape-- police,
crime, and death, green go on,
get out of hair.
Blonde, brunette, and red heads flare.
Snow white, black witch
reflects dark shadows in
green forest, on white snow, yellow candy rock
mountain, sky blue, red sunset,
gray clouds, white lightening,
bloodshot eyes.
Red eye train's already gone.
Green Hornet views yellow jacket, blue beetle,
red comet, blue lagoon, green dragon,
pink, white, and skin bunnies.
Green berets attack yellow sandy beaches, blue waters,

dark trenches. Multicolor flashes of fire
yield red blood,
white sheets,
fading light of life.
Gold stars red rage bury blue bellies
and yellow cowards.
Blue birds
and red cardinals fly
after white balls with red stitches.
Black and golds on fields are not related
to same colored penguins on ice.
On the outside, I am white,
top color ever changing, inner blue,
gray lead feet, brown eyes toting a golden heart.

Living Sign

I am the tall one, pure,

untouched by human forces.

I am someone special,

granted time and elements to flourish.

I am wounded, violated,

exploited by humankind.

I am transformed and reshaped,

worked into another something.

I am beautiful, scars healed,

replanted into another environment.

I am the symbol of a new time,

replaced a tarnished history.

I am the tree, I am me,

created for the world to see.

I am the past hidden self,

gifted with a whole new life.

Christmas Wreath

The stillness and solitude of the cold dark night is done,
    and I'm the evergreen branches rustling quietly in the morning sun.
The serene and calm environment is suddenly and painfully broken,
    as someone is taking me without a word being spoken.
From a magnificent tree that I once majestically did stand,
    now piled on the ground in bundles, my limbs tightly wrapped in a band.
I realize my coming fate and do yield with relief,
    for I have been picked to serve as a Christmas wreath.
Like a painter or sculptor, my creator was truly an artist.
    His design for me was considered one of the hardest.
But the skilled craftsman works quickly as his hands blend and mold.
    It doesn't take too long and I'm off to be sold.
Hung high in the display for all to see,
    I'm really so proud of what has been made of me.
Many look at my arrangement and wish I were more affordable,
    for my cost can only be paid by someone who thinks I'm most adorable.
Throughout the day I'm seen and admired by all,
    but as evening approaches, I'm still on the wall.
The day comes to a close and the door is locked,
    I try thinking of good things to keep my rejection blocked.
Then comes a figure out of the shadows of the night,
    It's the one they call Bobbi and she wonders if she doing what's right.
Her sons are bewildered as their discussions are many,
    their solutions are few while their problems are plenty.
She sees my beauty and quickly makes her selection,
    I'm to be a gift in a home where there is no rejection.
With great care in handling, I'm taken to meet this person who is most caring.

I learn it's her job to keep people's lives in a state that is more bearing.
I'm cheerful greeted and accepted with a gentle smile,
and then the two discuss their lives for a little while.
It seems they share a different bond as each has their own history,
but definite boundaries must be maintained which make sort of a mystery.
At last I hang on the door to greet friends from the present and the past,
each will receive by their act of giving so all want the holiday to last.
Here in this home where God still does linger and dwell,
old and new activities will become traditions for her children to tell.
Now my needles start to fall as Christmas is gone and I know the end is near,
but I've seen love and warmth and even a happy and joyful tear.
As I hear the bells ring from the distant church with the white steeple,
has my path been any different from what the Creator designed as people?

Pink Slippers

Light danced off the last quivering leaves,
    winter almost gone but hanging on,
cold breezes chilling the starless night.

Two windows illuminated, her bedroom lights
    filtered through brown tattered shades.
The house, old as the aged inhabitant,
    creaked, shivering without heat.

A preacher found her frozen body,
    fetally cuddled in her worn gown,
her dirty slippers, once pink and bright,
    flapping soles wrapped in worn silver tape.

Expressionless wrinkled face,
    gray hair straggled over a yellowed pillow,
she left alone, clutching bundles of hundred dollar bills,
  unacknowledged by the son
    who never came.

Sylvia's Path

Who are you and where?
Lead me! The avenue I must follow.
I need your caring, imagined
someone of mental illusion,
yet feeling no one there.

Your pathway of nothing,
light reflecting movement,
zombie motions, busy toys
of comfort, disconnecting persons,
different places, empty spaces.

Prayers petitioning, answers obscured,
seeking something, you look to night,
pills swallowed, smoke inhaled,
liquids consumed, relief a shadow,
today real, tomorrow a dark maybe.

Trapdoor triggering, a sad mind
opening, subject falling,
alternatives closing, emotions void,
period of selected loneliness,
a grave of buried memories.

Untouchable solutions floating
in blind spaces, seen
reality invisible, tears
clouding the vision of truth,
varnishing tales for tomorrow.

Life needs treasuring, death
the master, a second of metal
ending the torture. Hands
falling, missing the help,
landing heavy on others.

Crystals

Tears reply to a sparkle—
an image—
a diamond—one carat,
laid in white gold,
placed on my finger—
eyes blur in halos,
rainbows matching
the radiating rays
of a reflecting stone.
No announcement
of engagement
or coming marriage.
The ring-- a hard
earned trade
for work
that was
very masculine
in nature.
The tears-- symbols
of hard earned
and deserved
feelings of my
womanhood.

Ending

The pain of betrayal—shattered trust
seeking shadows of understanding void of words.

Loneliness plays in puddles of pity,
pitting warm tears against cold anger.

Disillusionment:
starting with an honest marriage,

Dedication:
recalling unselfish actions,

Dependence:
sacrificing a portion of one's self,

Desires:
yielding to another cause,

Depression:
winning over logic,

Dreams
ending in separation.

Time chasing—cherished memories—days in union—
stealing emotions while burying golden expectations.

Allegiance—grown children choosing,
sparking confusion of true caring.

The question clouding the couple's departure,
who owns these true and viable statements?

Little Creek

Bad decisions are like a small creek that flows
toward a body of settlement.
Eroding loosely rooted bonds and creating
depositions of isolated islands
that can't support growth.
Volume, building from connecting
sources and additional grades
provide a plunging ruin
toward a damaged destination.
No meandering but the direct approach
of authoritative supremacy slice
through ripples of respected imagines

once held in esteem,
now lead to a volley
of swelling pollution
in an ocean of regret.

UPJ Period

Geologic Vegetable Beef Stew

Winter's coming and the human body will need warm fuel,
Steaming geyser hot stew, it's about as healthy as you can get.

The following recipe comes straight from the enlightened theory,
The earth of a billion years old must have done something right.

The brackish brown ocean at night provides the base of our creation,
Put one gallon of this beef flavor mixture into a large cooking pot.

Your captured sea should be sitting on an earth's hot spot,
Don't make it an active volcano, keep the heat on low.

If you are a vegetarian, skip the next three couplets. They aren't for you,
What's going to happen next is not pretty and one you should avoid.

You island cannibals or cave dwelling species of human kind,
Find three pounds of fresh one-inch cubes of choice animal flesh.

Listen for screams when browning the carcass over a forest of hot flames,
The device holding the meat should have a quarter pound of butter.

Collect the morsels from the frying pan and place them in the warm ocean,
Watch the bubbles of death surface as you submerge their bodies.

Vegetarians may now return as the fun part for them is about to unfold,
Depending on your culinary pleasure, now line up all your spices.

Take a pinch of this, a douse of that and don't forget grandma's special,
When it comes to stew, geologic, Irish or other, anything goes.

Take an elongated folded mountain with long glacial striations,
Slice the specimen that resembles celery in one half-inch pieces.

Temporally store these gems of nature in a valley size bowl,
You will be given instructions when they will become deposits.

Select two representatives of the layers of all geologic time,
Cut these tear producers in half but don't rub your eyes.

Lay one half flat and slice eight moon shaped pieces,
Finish the job which will give you a count of thirty-two.

Let them rain into the depression container with their friends,
Next pull three large orange stalactites through the ground.
Dice these into gold coins that you could give away freely,
Help the eyes that they better see—that's no wife's tale.

Two dozen small asteroids just starting to turn coal red
Pick out their eyes but save and sever the red skin.

If the round shapes just mentioned are new and hard,
Let them simmer in the ocean that is presently bubbling.

Locate one yellow, two red and three green boulders with round sides,
Inside, cut away the beehive cluster of seeds and four web edges.

Cut into designs that suit your creative fancy but remain mouth-sized,
Be brave but don't cut your index finger as blood isn't an ingredient.

Agate clouds with tornado stems whose normal habitat is very dark,
	Slice them into pieces that resemble the scene of Hiroshima.

Scrap away yellow conchiodal humps from the long rows on an ear,
	Or just buy a sixteen-ounce package from the Green Giant.

Search for the fossil trail of the extinct chicken that was green,
	Pick up the long toes and short heels-cut off the tips and stems.

Enduring a snow storm of the sweet and tender variety,
	Collect enough pods to covers the same area as the above.

You cry for help in identification and amounts I forgot to list?
	Make the latter equal to the weight of the yellow kernels.

If I have to tell you the exact name of each item to use,
	You are definitely not an Irish geology major at UPJ.

Like the Niagara Falls, let your mountain of vegetables flow into the ocean,
	I usually put them by the handful to avoid a tidal wave on the stove.

Finally, pour one pint of the cream form The Big Rock Candy Mountain,
	Add with two cups of instant potato flakes—a cup of brandy if you like.

Cook on a simmering volcano until the crisp bite of hard vegetables is gone,
	But don't let this awesome and fantastic brew turn to a stew of mush.

You now have a batch of stew that will feed over twenty-one hungry people;
Have a party, treat neighbors or store in the freezer for a cold winter.

Falling

Feather, don't float, hurry,

catch the round steel ball.

Sky has no vacuum,

fall on your own.

Stop crying,

foul hates fair, find your nest.

The ball rolls to rest.

turns to rust then dust.

You are blown here,

and there, and everywhere.

No home you'll ever have,

foul defeats fair.

What's the moral to hear?

you're no tortoise,

the ball no hare.

Do you have a purpose?

Find your haven,

forget foul, think fair.

Float slowly, glide high,

sail softly, find a mission.

Fly feather fly,

sky be your heaven,

freedom be your master,

fill the air with care.

Difference

Men eating with men,

talk sports and women--

occasionally boast about business—

always jockeying for position--

are in competition—thinking

and offering solutions—

the correct way it needs to be done.

Secrets remain secrets.

Women eating with women,

discuss personal problems—

ears are rarely connected to the mouth—

it's a listening game

of understanding —feeling

each others inner emotions without

judgment or even suggestions.

Secrets are exposed.

I know these are facts

as I’ve sat at both tables.

Pleading guilty to indifference

at the first table—

finding absolution from gentle

voices at the opposite setting.

All human life eventually ends--

and so must my unusual journey.

Across the grave--on the good side--

never did any deeds worthy

of eternal flames--I’ll sit, float,

maybe fly—knowing

each species will be coming

to meet in discussion.

However then, we’ll know

all the answers.

Weekend

It's almost ten-thirty in the morning, Sunday—my deadline for leaving.
I could go late but it would mean missing activities
that for this pack-rat are needed.
Oil's checked and the exploding gas prices have been fully honored.
Heat's cut back, no toilet running, plants watered, stove's off,
refrigerator doors closed, lights out, just lock the door.
Locking insures I'll be able to prove
I've been robbed—nothing more.
Enough audio cassettes for today and to keep me awake on the return trip,
an Igloo container of frozen goodies I made for two days at work, security
uniform--don't forget the shoes—male oxfords--required—not very
feminine, candy for workers and visitors,
a case for security items, school materials and reading.
Check list says let's go—two days of my life each
week—five left for my interests.
The trip always starts with a tradition from the past—a prayer, now mental,
offered for safe passage. The environment of the four hour drive offers
changing scenes of excitement—animal life--see the hawk,
watch out for the skunk, and brake for the deer.
Beyond mother nature in her veils for each season—snow, rain, painted leaves,
green grass, outcrops, sprouting branches, and sunshine.
Relaxed, the first bargain store comes at the third hour, Lancaster—
treasures rarely exceed five dollars in price per item unless it's an
economic gem. Most of my purchases will end up on e-Bay sales.
CD's, books, toys, statues, vases, plates, souvenirs, and glassware for starters—
then come the clothes. Two closets of blouses and I keep buying more—a

feminine addiction. No shoes—my canoes are hard to find

An hour plus later, a stop at the outlet to buy donuts and cookies for the press workers who provide me ten different newspapers to read at night—I'm the guard at a printing facility. The next sales saving establishment, which sports better merchandise as it's in the "richie" area, gets more of my dollars. The taggers are minimum wage workers who don't know quality. This auctioneer has experience.

Finally, I visit my girlfriend, Casey, who lets me sleep at her house on Monday's. We chat while she works on her acres—sometimes I'm able to offer a lending hand. Then it's off to my place of employment.

From six in the evening to eight in the morning—fourteen hours, I stay awake with great effort near the end. I smile, say hello to Casey on my way to bed as she heads to work—she understands.

Four hours of sleep, I could use ten, and then I'm back on the road to visit my healer—thank God she's covered by insurance. I review my week's dilemmas and joys and always leave ready for the world. Another eight hours of work, four hours of driving through the night and then I'm back home.

Make assignment corrections for class,
sleep three hours and then off to UPJ—
tired but smiling.

"I" with Eyes

If "I" of me had eyes to see,

what would eyes see in me?

Eyes can see but not speak

so eyes' words are not heard.

But if eyes could speak her peace,

eyes would make a long speech,

savoring many things to say.

Eyes might soothe my sadness,

if she could solve certain sorrows.

Eyes would be cautious yet clever

to tell of tales that I'd approve.

Eyes could be tempted to tell

tiny secrets others would enjoy,

but she'd test the waters of my mind

before treading beyond the tidal shore

Thus it really does not matter if

        "I' has eyes to totter in talk,

As eyes and "I" are never apart.

Ten Blessings of Roberta

I. I am Roberta,

blessed as a woman

with integrity, self-love, and love for humankind

II. I am Roberta,

blessed as a human being

in the Greater Scheme of things.

III. I am Roberta,

blessed with a respect

for a Higher Power in creation.

IV. I am Roberta,

blessed to be given

the free will of worship

V. I am Roberta,

blessed to have been born

of intelligent parents who planned for my future.

VI. I am Roberta,

blessed by not yielding

to the murder of myself or another.

VII. I am Roberta,

blessed with three beautiful children,

now adults, from one legal spouse in marriage.

VIII. I am Roberta,

blessed with physical and mental abilities to

earn an honest living.

IX. I am Roberta,

blessed to have been taught to

speak the truth.

X. I am Roberta,

blessed with all the necessary things for survival and

the choice to find another with the loss of the first.

Change

Growth in body increases a size, growth in mind doesn't change
cell number in the mind, growth in acceptance
increases self-confidence and mental stability.
He has reached a peak in stature and as age increases,
the body is slowly reversing back to right field,
having played many positions in the game of life.
I was four feet, eight inches, grew to five feet,
nine and one half inches. Now I am only
five feet, eight and one half inches. Where did the
important inch at twenty-one years of age go?
He sees the need to investigate the elements of knowledge,
the horse finally sees the water and the need to drink,
he saddles education as his vehicle to advancement.
The greatest growth came in she emerging from he, the hidden
self that needed to be released, gives birth to
fulfillment of life—being the person one was meant to be.

I looked to the seminary for the truth to my doubts,

only to find more questions than answers.

She advances in wisdom as the years now stack one upon the other,

the world doesn't stop to take notice of her but she of it,

wisdom always leading to the final truth of another question.

I have struggled for truth in other areas but the

greatest dealt with who I am. Recognizing the

need to be the real me placed barriers and

destroyed many established relationships.

Society has difficulty in accepting the fact

that I learned to accept myself.

Escaped

Lone footprint
dried in mud,
violation of the ground,
evidence
of someone
unwanted by police,
cutting corners,
on a hurried journey.
Hard concrete
sidewalk
left no message,
where
the suspect of nothing
has gone.

Gateway

I feel the cold that was warmth this morning.
It tocuhes me and grabs the ground
It jumbles the surrounding air everywhere,
confusing the mix into a mist creating fog.
The visible sky takes flight and disappears,
leaving a blank white nothing ahead,
behind, and above — a cloud fallen to earth.

I don't salute or rebuke the intruder,
whose moisture dampens my face and woolen coat,
dissolving real surroundings into forged patterns.
I walk through the screen of haze without fear,
engulfed in my own world of disturbing thoughts.
Nothing moves as there is nothing there,
no bell tower to chime the time or designate my setting.

An outside is intermingling with the inside of my mind,
both converging into a single hole of isolation:
the gateway to imagined rejections and imposed self-pity.

Ode to Alessandra

I write, she answers,
“Story poem—yes, it does stand on its own!
Vivid and powerful message.”
I submit, she replies,
“Wonderfully imaginative poem. Gives insight to the speaker’s

frame of reference, experiences, background and wishes."

I compose, she counters,
“I whiff the subtle Roethke—winds in the words.
Intriguing weave of nature and spiritual concerns.”
I revise, she responses,
“Send this one to the newspaper! Spread the word!” I
author, she acknowledges,
“This is a poem about value and being devalued.”
I struggle, she offers empathy.
“You often enjoy the strategy of questioning to pull the
reader in, cause her to reflect a self outside the poem.” I
confess, she reflects hope,

“I truly hope you have the opportunity to share
this with a larger audience and spread the word.”
I shape, she helps design,
Your story illustrates the photograph perfectly! I think there is
enough material here to unfurl into a full-fledged novel should you
have the inclination (and time)! Intriguing—esp. towards the end
when you really speak/write from the mind of the main character.
There’s definitely a movement from the external—Enjoyable read.
I create, she agrees,
“Bravo! I can feel the ache of a speaker in this poem.
It picks up passion through the questions on the second page.
Vivid descriptions throughout. Feels like a real emergence.”
I say “Thank You”, she smiles, accepting the gratitude.

The First

Am I the first to touch and treasure this earthy spot—

contaminating it for the next human who follows?

Scorpions, snakes, rodents or who knows what creatures

might have wiggled, walked, slithered or stalked the area.

But could I be the first on this spot in a vast desert, what a thought.

What if, what if I were really the first since creation!

Oh, this desert was once an inland ocean, how about fish?

Fish! One can't forget the turtles, sponges and the squid.

Thousands of swirling snails and what of the number of dead--

the space could be the burial grounds of those billions that floated.

But could I be the first on this spot in a vast desert, what a thought.

What if, what if I were really the first since creation!

The Native Americans, early settlers or ones who cross the straits

could have rested their tired bodies where I am standing.

Their children might have played here and the buffalo did roam.

But could I be the first on this spot in a vast desert, what a thought.

What if, what if I were really the first since creation!

My kind has only lived a tiny fraction of the time in years

hat the dinosaurs inhabited and dominated the earth.
They left tracks, bones and eggs buried in million year layers.
But could I be the first on this spot in a vast desert, what a thought.
What if, what if I were really the first since creation!
A bird, buzzard or even an eagle might have chosen to land
where I harbor to be the first. Could a mere dropping from the air
stake claim before I—No! It has to be alive and of some species.
But could I be the first on this spot in a vast desert, what a thought.
What if, what if I were really the first since creation!
But what if, what if I really were the first since creation—the very first?
The dignity of such a notation leans toward the sacred.
The purest link between time, humankind and a Higher Power
rest in my existence as I stand in humble awe of my privilege.
If there is a soul in my body, does it cry, "I am even closer?"

Trumpet Player

We are close, the conductor raising baton,

my hands, trained, initiate the concert.

The silver lips of my trumpet are glossy and cool,

they receive my trained tongue.

I finger the hard peaks of pulsating beats,

gentle strokes creating muted sighs.

The scale mounts then intervals of chords force

the notes' pressures to arouse and tease.

Sharps pierce the levels of comfort,

flats take it down, down to acceptance.

The overture of my performance is classical

by developing harmony in the pursuit of a finale.

I receive a standing ovation

allowing admission for penetrating pleasure.

The music raises and lowers in octave rhythm

to a taut tightening toward a crescendo.

Interluding with a smile, scattering the sheets,

my audience of one applauds and cries-- encore, encore.

Words

Words created for ears to hear,
words coined to carry narrations,
words critiqued by puzzled peers,
words penned to be poetry.
Words musing into metaphors,
words shaping similes like sonnets
words showing tales of telling,
words penned to be poetry.
Words packed with private meaning,
words flat and scripts of nothing,
words wordy and stuffed with errors,
words penned to be poetry.
Words rejected by degreed tutors,
words sailing past wanted readings,
words sinking before buoys of books,
words penned to be poetry.
Words craving written acceptance,
words mounting in a wake of waiting,
words, words, so many words,
words penned to be poetry.

Summer Writing Programs

Old Upright

Heavy and bulky, the antique piano's aging wood

hides a vessel of strings secured to cast metal.

Black piers anchored among chipped ivory.

Seating bench harbors tattered sheets of time.

Agile fingers dance a tap and toe on selected surfaces,

triggering a roll of wooden rods,

forcing felted hammers of stretched wires,

yielding agony from screaming chords.

Three brass feet shoed by one guiding foot

chain musical waves from escaping,

breaking their expected departure, then releasing,

like fading ripples on a quiet pond.

Notes scribing melodies, skeletons of days long forgotten,

blending cries into rhythms for human hearing,

memories swirling and resonating sounds,

mysterious mouth mythically speaks from nowhere.

Nothing Poem

Eyes gazing at nothing,
hypnotized
by blank white paper.

A pen,
dangling between the thumb and finger,
slowly scribbles.

Rising chest falling like old bellows,
rivals
a long streaking scratch—
a line of rejection,
then silence.
A thought,
lighting,
quickly sensing dark,
disappears.
A page of forced nothings!
A spark,
something sounding right,
tinders burning
thrills within,
flames licking,
heat mounting,
blazes flashing
the fire flowing

No time for retreat,
continue stoking of writing,
rolling lines like moving steel ,
riveting words to the page.

Relaxing,
breathing lightly,
hot coals settling into glowing embers.

Quiet Time

I came to the waters on the shore to renew threads,

to return to solitude with the Lady. The scene is simple—

the ocean adjoining the land draped in sunshine.

I sit on one of the stone fences lined like keys on a piano,

guards that protect the beaches from erosion.

At the edge of the breaking waters,

the eastern sun warms my aging face,

the western breeze chills my covered neck.

Morning has just drowned the darkness of the night.

The horizon splits the sky from ocean.

The dark blue waters at the line of division fade into light

green at my feet--the dark blue air dissolving into crystal white.

Time becomes lost in the motion, silence is the sound

of breaking waves. Lazy waves splash against the rocks

polishing their surfaces to a smooth finish.

Witness the war zone between the land and ocean,

cresting waves crash—lashing their anger on what won't

strike back. Sand charges forward but retreats next.
Tiny creatures perish--battered victims in the turbulent struggle.
Snake-like waters leap to escape their imprisoned basin.
I make a cross of the loose coins in my jacket. A quarter in the center,
dimes at the edges, two cents between the silver of the arms and the top,
five pennies in the bottom. The images' equals seventy-six cents.
Seventy six—the American symbol of freedom. Does the cross symbolize a
greater representation? Who needs to be freed? The lady sitting by the ocean?
Which way to face this symbol? Is the ocean the enemy or does the land
need saving? How long can this holy design remain? Will it last through
one storm, two or many? The changing tide could take it this evening.
Which way is it moving at the present? What would be lost? A child's
dream of riches could be fulfilled in an instant.
The ocean is deep, stirring, seeking, escaping but without understanding.
Am I a pebble on the beach--a grain of sand—a molecule in the ocean?
Is this the beach of the purity and innocence of youth
destroyed by winds and raging waters during adolescence?

Does the cross serve as a foundation for tomorrow?

I don't expect to see God come walking on the waters.

I need to climb the sandy hillside back to my own sea.

Walk a pathway listening to words coming from a similar ocean—

one spirited by the Divine. I need to be living—a survivor

swirling with the soul of light in the death of darkness.

Sonnet of Simplicity

Tarnished orange of autumn's withering leaf,
gently gliding over pasture's tan grass,
falling to earth without plan or belief,
harboring no facets of ugly crass.
Budded in light to life but leaf to die,
season spent as part of canopy's shade,
sharing this space but unaware of why,
now colorful cover to wade and fade.
All of nature follows this simple course,
plant or animal, leaf or humankind,
come and go, creating joy then remorse,
whether one celled or with creative mind.
Existence is a life exhausted here.
Dwellers their own purposes have to hear.

Day

Gray dawn morning surrenders to rising sun,

shadows of stretching limbs cradling the earth,

tiger lilies shedding their tears from cool night,

valley brook washing away the mist of fog,

breeze setting fields of wheat in swaying motion,

freezing, then darting, the hare moving in flight,

song birds announcing day by breaking silence,

my eyes tracing the trial of Day's blooming way.

Maureen

One Lonely Horse

As a young colt, I know I was bred from lines of a champion stock,

However, I really don't like being a mare with the body of a stud.

The pasture of my youth is spacious and flowing in green growth,

But Mother seems busy with others while Pop is always gone.

I am not expected to race or jump-just stay out of trouble while in the field,

At night and during bad weather, the barn offers shelter but no real love.

Like biblical Joseph of Egypt, I end up in a strange land not of my choosing,

The change opens new gates to learning while I view the future coming.

I use my new education to gain a passage way into new environments,

I mix with others and I find the special mate of my liking who is caring.

Three new colts emerge and grow while their parents slowly drift apart.

One day I am loaded on a trailer to be transported into another pasture.

The large space is lonely but the next field has a single mare so different,

She is younger by a few years but really knows how to care and listen.

I take to her consoling as I eat the greener grass on her side of the fence,

I enjoy her to the point that she means more to me than my own mother.

When I first come to this place, only two strands of barbed wire separate us,

As time passes, additional barbs are added making my nibbling difficult.

Large trees and shrubs grow up around her barn so I can no longer see it,

She distantly now grazes in the far end of the field next to another fence.

Today the wires are many and the horse in the pasture doesn't seem real,

Has a camouflaged statue with a recorded voice now taken her place?

In pain, I turn to find a quiet spot to cry when I notice the farmer's mistake,

The gate to my pasture has been left open. Is it time for me to bolt and run?

Surrogate Mother

You touched the inner self of her
who was not your carried baby,
with something she needed
to fill a void in her youth.

You stand, a forced distance,
untouchable, held by bonds
of your profession and
ties to your very own.

You are kind, a woman
with a spiritual pillar that
cares for hearts of youth
and suffering humans.

Once a year, your special day
as a bearer of children,
lost souls who wander, can
wish you the same as your own.

Broken Barriers

An empathic therapist and a mother of two, who
guided her own children into adulthood, sits
with an aging woman, seventeen years her senior.
It's their final session before Christmas and a new year.

The psychologist has caringly watched her client
over sixteen years take slow forward steps resulting
in both failure leading to growth and success
in remolding a former gender-troubled identity.

The caregiver has selected a children's book
as one of her Christmas gifts for this woman.
Snuggling next to each other, the words are read
by the giver that flood the mind of the receiver.

The magic of the story and the teller's tone, the spirit of a
Higher Power, and the rescue of a lost emotion, initiates
tears that meander down a wrinkled cheek as the elder's
inner child quietly cries aloud, "Would you hold me?"
The embrace breaks the chains of isolation from
life-long issues once locked in mental darkness

The Lady

An audience with hands clapping,
feet stomping,
voices cheering,
an occasional shrill whistle,
expressed their accepting elation for the couple's performance.
The artist acknowledged the tribute with pride.
The stage darkened with a focusing light on the lady,
she was offering an encore in appreciation.
A glance at the guitarist issued the instructions,
the ambiance of the crowd was hushed in anticipation.
A red gown with silver sequins traced her movement.
glossed burnt auburn eyelids closed and head lowered,
signaling a preparation for the coming selection.
Her husband meticulously chose the strings to vibrate
as the sounds found freedom in the vast arena of space.
All eyes, expect the infant asleep in a mother's arm,
oriented on the figure about to create another memory,
but they waited, waited quietly,
like vintage wine resting toward maturity.
This flavor could be sweeter as this time was ripe for gratification.
Her voice started with almost a whisper, slowly finding
sounds that stepped higher to another voice of music
but retreating like a gentle wave in a salty sea.
I heard what may not have been heard by others, the agony of
reminiscence, something buried deep in her past.
I don't know the anguish but I know her. The pain was visible.
Her recollection is a factor that helps her understand
the grief, suffering, and distress of others.
As she reached her peak of vocal expression,
the notes carried part of that hurt away.
Her song is finished until another show.

Happy Daughter Poem

Growing into womanhood
and out of adolescence,
I need the guidance
of a caring mother.
Accepting unwanted advice
is the growth from counsel
I hear her cheerful voice that
understands a young girl's dilemma.

Replacing loneliness
with hopefulness,
I take an affectionate hand.
Building confidence in a garden
where inferiority
grows like wild weeds,
I want this cultivator
who spreads seeds of assurance.
Fertilizing a daughter's creativity
while controlling
the wildness of her youth,
I sense a mother
who knows the difference.
Hiding her personal pain
and problems,
I let her dry my tears
while honoring the heart
of a gifted and giving woman.
Harvesting traits,
seeded and hoed by your efforts,
I recognize these fruits
displayed like hero's medals

Smiling you should know
that you've done your best.
I now say to you,

Happy Valentine's Day, Mom,
even if you're only
a super surrogate mother.

Lament on a Premature Termination

My eyes cried,
My fingers tingled,
My hands wrote,
My feet shuffled,
My ears listened,
My mouth requested,
My touch numbed,
My mind blanked,
My logic suffered,
My feelings longed,
My heart softened,
And then,
I said good-bye.

An Empty Chalice

Born as one, she and I, we grew together in flowered fields and the imaginary world within a sandbox until a nun on the 1st day of school left her in the front of the room with girls and dragged me to the back with those bully bunch of boys. I learned gender had boys and girls.

I couldn't see her anymore after that first day in school: only in my mind but she is always there. My mother wasn't around to help me with answers and my daddy was off to war-gone. We were alone and there we stayed. I grew without her but she waited for me to return.

Grade school was confusing. My subconscious still raises its ugly head on occasions to remind me of my stupidity planted by nun's chastising. The raggedy boys played in the dirty alley and learned survival. I was tough. Girls enjoyed protection from the nuns during dainty sidewalks games.

I found women who temporarily filled the void of loneliness she and I experienced. She talked to Lady and cried the day the car killed our dog. She helped me throw stones at cars one night in revenge. She hid the 2 years the priest abused me but came back when he left.

She shared my college and marriage years. She watched my 3 sons grow and my wife and I grow apart. The time came for us to be partners as one sex. We knew the decision was correct. We live together but still need to be of one mind. A 7 and 78 year old traveling in one body isn't right.

Is this fragile life shell of confusion the result of a flawed marriage by a father's affair, a mother's abandonment, a shredded gender identity sail, or the priest's torpedo of sexual abuse? Can it be the inability to escape past memories like a struggling swimmer drowning entangled in thick seaweed?

In 2 years, Cameli's and my counselor of 19 years will leave to enjoy her retirement on Cape Cod. Since we have united as women, we've come to the realization that we both are kneeling at the railing of life waiting for the communion of adulthood. I, Cameli, need to be me.

Presently, our mentor stands holding the chalice of knowledge that contains the host of my transformation. As she approaches, a force halts her movement. Something needs completed before these two can mature into one. A question remains, "What needs to be repaired?"

Physical things break and can be repaired. Surgeons can mend and replace body parts. We are dealing with a human mind that has been injured. It's difficult to bandage or replace damaged emotions. Determining what isn't functioning is a step forward. We have 19 months to sift 17 years of effort.

Later Years and Myself

Time Shift

Life belongs to here and now.
Past is gone, future will be.
I am me.
See me as I am.
Days will pass, end will come,
I will cease to write a word.
Will I be me or something else,
somewhere else, or simply gone?
Truth is fiction in a mind set,
time changes, so must I and I
will move on to another... another
unknown tomorrow with no questions.
Dark or light, heaven or hell,
creature or dust, more hidden truth.
Can I tell you of what I know
that is a void to me?
Day continues until night.
Beyond cannot be seen.
Who is to judge my pathway
when these footprints are gone?

My Space and Place

I am in this place, a space with accepting walls.
        I relive my past in number twelve Ariel black letters
carefully spreading out on pages of white paper,
    words are nerve impulses to my fingers
from a mind that struggles to remember long ago,
the time I was alone, the time I was abused,
    the time I knew I needed to be a different me, a she.

The closing line of my memoir opens the next page
        of another day's tomorrow until a sheet with nothings
spells that I am gone and my story starts eroding.
    What lines will be written between now and then can only be
    imagined, like novels of created fiction, poetry with daydreams
coming to life, or fate giving rise to a mirage,
lettering a better version of what I failed to see in previous light.

Journey in Poland

Can what she said really be true?
Some people have faith in miracles.
I'm not a betting woman,
but anything can blossom.

Spring opens doors of vegetation.
I don't have to believe, it happens.
But what she said requires …
requires a something special.

I've seen sunsets over canyons,
moonlight on mountains, love in light.
Her idea is a desert, a vast span
without substance for sustaining.

I have the need, the longing inside of me,
the missing link from childhood to aging adult.
The minister said as she smiled at me,
"Accept His hand on this troubled journey"

Age

It means nothing, purely and absolutely nothing

in the very beginning. Starts with pampering

and enjoying being fed—no clocks or calendars

to schedule anything—one's demands are met.

Exploration begins but responsibility is limited.

Listen, learn the simple rules of family living.

Time begins to take shape—special days

mean gifts and singled out attention.

Anticipation of Christmas and birthdays

lodges Hallmark events of passage.

Growth awakes the sense of measuring time,

adolescence to legal age really drags.

With experience, maturity molds to fashion,

a transition from acceptance to investigation.

Age melts like candles on a cake. Time reverses gears

at age twenty-one: forward shifts to high.

Forty, old as a teenager, is shuffled to fifty

when forty is in range. Forty approaches fifty,

if one is lucky and stays healthy, the bar lowers to sixty

--eventually lowering to the bottom.

Tiring bodies assume control of youthful minds.

Courage defies quitting as strength labors.

Memories travel positive pathways. Old becomes a virtue.

Happiness anchors at ports for future generations.

Life is going to end—no way to avoid the issue.

Whether young or in the twilight of existence,

make each day settle by finding pathways

that spirit the aging heart.

Getting Old

Something … sound… noise,,, strange noise…
from where… what is it?
Casual awareness, sleep ending, day starting---the alarm!
Regretful buzzing, only reachable with left arm for people
who sleep on their side and keep the metal rooster
on the right side of the bed.

I could move the night stand to the opposite side of the bed
but then I couldn't sit on the edge of the bed
to drag things out of the vanity.

Everything has its price.
The left shoulder suffers from arthritis,
so the semi-conscious reaction
sends the shock of pain to the brain.

Ouch! It's morning.
Hit the snooze and return to the land of nothing.
After three quick nine minutes of peace in earthly bed,
the light and alarm win the battle.

I decide to give up and get up.
I flip the covers to the left, ouch, another shock.
I swing my legs toward the edge and let the legs
drop to place on the floor…next to slippers.
Arms gently lift the right leg and apply one slipper.
Seven years ago the doctor told me,
"You tell me when, Lady."
A new knee? He may be ready, but I am not.
The mental war between me and consent is always greater
when I see the doctor twice a year for my physical.
When I can no longer walk,
if I am alive,
I'll give it a shot…but only then.

I move to the upright position and view the room.
Nothing is changed, the mess is still there.
No little critters, fairies, or elves doing secret work at night.
Maybe today but surely by tomorrow, I'll do my womanly thing.

I grab a pair of panties and head for the bathroom.

I never understood
    why they called them a pair or the plural: panties,
        when there is only one item.
            Yes, two legs go through them.
Maybe it has something to do with a belly and a butt.

Into the bathroom, I pull up the knob in the tub
    and turn on the hot water,
        add softener, body oil, and bubble bath.

I stop at the sink and brush my teeth making sure
    that I don't keep too much foaming paste in my mouth
        when I go after the back molars
            that it causes me to gag.
                I hate it when that happens.
Next I park on the potty
    and deposit yesterday's meals
        plus last night's beer and snack.
I wash my hands even though I am about to take a bath.
            I have a few other chores to complete
                as the tub takes a while to fill.
I blow my nose for the first time
    and then assemble the pills from four prescriptions
that contribute to keeping me in the face of others—
    high blood pressure
        high cholesterol,
            female hormones,
                and anxiety,
                    commonly called depression.

I also take woman's vitamins,
vitamin C,
        calcium,
                a long named pill that is supposed to help my knee,

                    I'd have to check the spelling, and lysine—
  that keeps one from getting cold sores.

        I really hate those things.

It's like walking around with a giant mushroom
stuck to your face.

Next, I descend the stairs while holding on to the banister
with the right hand while the left holds the pills in the left palm
secured with three fingers while the thumb and index finger
grasp the dish from last night's snack
that I ate when I watched a video.

I've lost three plates this past year doing this balancing act.
I should move downstairs now that mother is gone.
It would be safer---
especially in case of a fire.

It would likely mean bringing out
the forty-four Smith and Wesson
with hollow points
as there is an outside entrance in her bedroom.

I just think that I'll stay upstairs
with the twenty-two Ruger.

I stop in the kitchen to put the plate in the sink
if I still have it
and set the medication on the counter.
Yesterday, I wasn't quite awake
and came downstairs carting my clean panties
instead of the plate.

Once a week I lose one of the pills
and have to back track up the steps looking for the tiny thing.
I once looked for five minutes only to find a pink droplet stuck
to the inside of my palm from the moisture
left when I washed my hands.
You do remember that I washed my hands after visiting the toilet.
I take the pills with a small glass of orange juice—breakfast.

Blow my nose
and then go to mom's room to turn on the computer,
space heater, and electric track that has the stereo attached.

Blow my nose again—
I don't know, maybe I've developed allergies this past year.
It's not a cold.

I climb back up the steps to the second floor
and check the water level in the tub.

Water comes out very slowly on the second floor.
It does the same thing on the first floor
but we're not talking about that floor now.
I turn on the CD player to high volume,
return to the bedroom
where I strip,
like in naked,
and then return to the bathroom.

I turn off the faucet
and test the solution
by dipping my toes into the water.
I usually have the temperature just right.
I step in, sit down, and then lean back
as the water rises to the tub's edge
but doesn't overflow.

I lie there enjoying the warmth
and the music
until the water level finishes seeping out of the overflow.
I then sit up, shampoo,
wash my body
while letting the tub again fill to the overflow level.
I apply conditioner
and sink back to the resting state.
After about ten minutes of relaxing,
I reach up with my big toe and push down the plunger
to release the water from the tub.
When the water is gone,
I sit up and rinse my hair.
Getting up and getting out
has become a minor problem.
A battle exists each morning (I rarely bathe at night)
between the right knee and the left shoulder
as to which body part is going to suffer the least
in the weird manipulation
to escape the vessel
and land on a dry floor.

I always think of the late pope

who fell and broke his leg
while getting out of the tub.
I can't imagine
an aide coming to the assistance
of a naked pope.

I will install a set of safety bars
and gain a little exercise practicing my moves
on the Jungle Jim while obtaining an upright position.
Towel the hair and wipe the body gently stepping out—
another bar will be needed.

Quickly blow my nose
as the heat has loosened a cascade of dripping stalactites.

Put on my waiting panties
and head for the bed edge in the next room.
Snap on my bra in the front.
I can no longer reach behind to do the job
and twisting the thing from front to back
and then getting into the harness
is out of the question.

Bras and women run a changing history.
The excitement starts when walnuts surface
that begin to harden into lemons
that yielded to delicate peaches,

then on to hot tomatoes.

Children aided the development of cantaloupes

but few ever made melons.

Now I scoop up my crooked-necked squashes

and plop them into the pockets of my bra

and gently arrange a desired shape.

Next the legs await recognition.

Starting with the right, I apply lotion to the feet and leg

and slip on the special stockings to relieve

the dilemma of heavy varicose veins,

but being careful not to remove the prescription cream

that I placed in the hole in my leg

where they did the biopsy

when I had a collapsed vein.

Left leg doesn't demand any attention

other than the application of a lotion.

It will likely be the one that has the clot

that kills me just to get special attention.

Slide into the slacks, return the slippers to their masters

and overhead a blouse.

Back to the bathroom,

stop to blow the nose,

add drop drops of sheen to the damp,

not damn hair, and brush out the tangles.

Comb the locks straight,

clean the deposits from the comb

and drop the mess into the toilet.

No need to flush, wait until later.
Blow dry and curl the bangs.

Apply pearl shadow to the eyelids

and a natural shade in hiding the dark circles below.

Moisturize skin and let massacre complete the job.

I only apply lipstick when I reach my destination of somewhere,

wherever that may be.

Deodorize the under arms,

squirt a few puffs of perfume

behind the ears and on the breast.
Back down the stairs with purse on shoulder.

Check the computer for e-mails,

(Peace out to you Sister will be there, but she's not my sister)

and news while listening to piano music or a favorite singer.

Pack the knapsack on wheels,

grab fudge for friends on campus,

exchange slippers for boots in winter—shoes in summer.

Scarf and jacket complete the final chore.

Purse in hand,

making very sure the keys are there.

Yes. I've locked myself out-- at least twice a year.

Step outside dragging the different loads.

Slam the locked door and then greet the world.

It looks like the Lord

has granted me another day.

One Act Play

The curtain opened, no applause, yet
I introduce myself, spanked
by a doctor's hand, the nurse
in white, penciled in my beginning.

Breath wavered, eyes bulged,
body tensed, my mind in awe.
When I grow up, I want to be,
I'm going to be just like that.

From toddler to teen,
it depended on the day,
the person I met, the movie
I saw, the game I played.

I never wanted to go to school,
be a nun, or Jesus on the cross,
but a figure skater, a baseball player,
the street car conductor,

a screen star, the lady at the toy counter,

dreams tip toeing into my tomorrow.

I grew up and reached the stage

where all players perform,

seeking another horizon

in anticipation of childhood wonder.

I learned new games and managed,

becoming adept at what I did.

I was busy, auditioning many roles,

trying to prove the lines suited my part,

the drama of each day

announced the beat of my drum,

orchestrating a litany of lyrics

I'd sing to experience a rewarding applause.

I grew like all actors,

flourishing in the arena of activity.

Like a plant becoming dry with age,

nature responds to my last flowering,

I yearn to live the part I never played,

the lost thrill of that childhood awe,

yet I watch a young performer feel

my role,

the one I never found the chance to dance.

Song of My True Self

If Walt can sing praises to himself, why can't I?
While he was content to voice a song in singular,
I will take the occasion of dealing double.
I will not pretend to be special but really, I am.
My kind of gender is one in ten thousand,
a type that drives loving and sweet mothers to tears
and fills masculine fathers with bitter contempt.

If you are interested in the good life, this isn't it.
You'll hide from yourself and lie to others,
achieve feats of manly wonder that draw hate
from the real species who struggle to equal
your accomplishments that really mean nothing—
action raised to lower suspicions from a sterile society.

What you see depends on when you looked.
At fifteen, I stood four feet, eight inches of skin and bones,
more bones than skin with very little muscle.
You would have put me in right field and prayed.
That's where I always was anyway and prayers didn't help.

But if I lost my shorts while chasing the ball I missed, you'd
see two I never had to catch—they came with the package.
They were society's label that I was a boy—hung from the start.
But if I fell, broke my stick, and cracked open my head,
the breasts without a bra inside my head would flop out
and take an infield position and would startle the crowd

and that would definitely make me a girl without a bat.

The game never came where that happened so I stayed
the same except the testosterone came and played
a different sport that inflated my body to five feet,
nine inches that posted me as a beer drinking, always right,
sports nut, money hungry, womanizing, mother fuckin' man.
No, they're not all like that but why take chances.

I wanted out, and outted someday I would be. I didn't make it
soon enough as testosterone, remember him, caught me
off guard and I ended up married to one of my own
and we put three new humans on the planet.

I once read that time cures all difficulties. However,
the idiot who initiated the saying forgot to finish
the statement. Time does cure all problems but
creates new dilemmas, maybe even worse
than the original pile of crap one was sitting in.

I figured out how to get the best of testosterone, I'd cut
him off, turned him inside out and made him a vagina.
I can't wait until the day comes when I find my dream boy
who penetrates my body and spits in his face.
To make matters worse for him, he'll be the
instrument of my fulfilling, breath-taking female orgasm.

Yes, I am now the half that I needed to be. Sir, you
can now call me Madam, or by my original name, it's easy,

I only added an "a." You can handle that and don't forget
to tip your hat while opening the door for me.
I'm a lady, a beautiful lady, and don't you dare say I'm not,
even if I am loud and aggressive. I've got the right
hardware, in the right places, and don't you forget it.

I really enjoy being me and with my kind. I am able to talk
about real things those men don't discuss. I can tell you
when I am sad, need nurturing, and you listen, just listen.
That's all, that's what I need for you to do, just listen.
You know that, you're a woman. I don't need the all out
detailed solution to a dilemma that men give me that
they know nothing about but can't lower their pride to admit.

Now, if you see me sitting alone at the local bar,
you've likely made a mistaken in identity as I don't go there.
But if you did see me and knew it is me outside the bar,
chances are you wouldn't be someone from my youth
because only a few on my old buddies know the truth
and the others are dead—passed on while I transitioned,
but if you do see me and know it's me, say hello and
greet me with a smile that I will return because
I'm a very happy teenage girl. I just turned thirteen.

That is only mental but I'm really growing up twice.
Since I taught giddy girls at thirteen for thirty years,
I've eliminated that stage of my development.
But I can imagine their girlish thoughts of me,
their childish efforts seeking my attention

while I was equally thriving on theirs.

I didn't assign seats but let their choices unfold.
It ended the same way, year after year,
pretty and intelligent girls in front, the middle mixed
in awe, and the, "I don't give a damns' in the back.
The shuffle and fight for the front did change,
motivational prizes for the best and most improved,
aroused and opened eyes of the "could be goods,"
who left ninth grade with an interest they didn't
know they had when they originally came that fall.

But that was then and this is now, they're gone.
I take their places in the classrooms on campuses,
struggling to deal with lost parents, a pedophile priest,
and a boy named Robert from my past that must be told.
Yet delighting in a growth that each new poem stirs
and lifts another pain to paper to be recorded,
exposure to be examined in the light of understanding,
words exhuming damage then erasing ugly scars.

The tomorrows that come before the black shovels in,
are racing toward a goal to another horizon
that appeared when death delivered a void space
in the dying town of my birth and beginning.
I will not let the chained ball
keep me from climbing to a height where
my treasure box of contentment waits me.

The view on the trail behind me leaves footprints,
only mine, but I see the strangers standing beside the path,
they were the those whose words picked me up,
offered me a drink of wisdom, and nudged me forward
toward the top, one after one, they were there.

End

About the Author

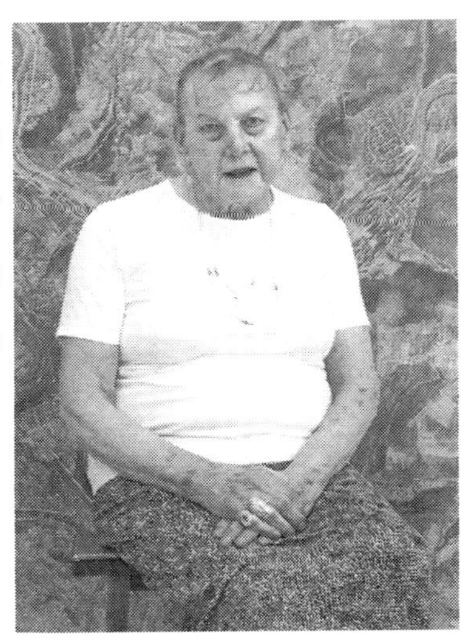

Robert Clayton Dostal was born on Thanksgiving Day in 1934. The first five years of his life were spent living in the country at Good's Corner ncar the city of Johnstown. He seemed to challenge his parents or caretaker by wondering off to explore the countryside and its surroundings.

In 1939, his parents had a martial problem that ended up with Robert being sent to a family friend's home until the issues were resolved. One of the dilemmas that occurred was his family home was lost and eventually a house in East Conemaugh was purchased. In this community Robert would attend the Sacred Heart Grade School before moving on the Johnstown Catholic High School.

Robert would be the first to admit that school was a place that he hated to attend. Interest in academic studies wasn't on his radar screen the entire trip through the eight grades. Robert made it through the system largely due to the fact that his father, a doctor who took care of the priests and nuns for free, was one of the highest donators at Sacred Heart Church.

Johnstown Catholic High School, now Bishop McCort, wasn't much different to Robert. It was in ninth grade that fate would deal this youngster a severe blow. The main building in Roxbury wasn't big enough to hold all of the incoming freshmen. It was Robert's misfortune to be assigned to St. John's Gualbert Annex. A Catholic Salesian priest assigned to the parish who taught the religious classes turned out to be a pedophile and Robert was one of his victims.

After the 9th grade, Robert would be taken by the pedophile on a summer religious journey to The Shrine of Sainte-Anne-de-Beaupré, located near Québec City in Canada. Since Robert wasn't being a very cooperative product for his use, this abusive priest would convince the boy's parents that the child's poor behavior would be resolved if the boy were sent to a boarding school. After attending a summer camp at the Salesian facility in Goshen, New York, the youngster would be sent to a Salesian School in New Rochelle, New York. Still a problem child, Robert was sent to Don Bosco Agricultural High School in the mountains located some distance from the small village of Huttonsville in West Virginia.

This school's activities and academic program would help Robert finally head toward becoming a maturing young adult. He excelled in sports, academics, and was popular among the students and faculty. Robert avoided seeing the priest during winter vacations and took a summer job on the school's farm so he would not have to return to Johnstown. In the summer of 1953, the priest returned to Italy and wasn't given a visa to reenter to the United States. Robert knows that he wasn't the only victim of this priest because the wolf in Shepard's clothes would often say to Robert, "Why aren't you as cooperative as the other boys that I see."

Robert was accepted to Penn State University where he graduated four years later as a teacher of Vocational Agricultural and General Science. While at Penn State, Robert became a leading figure in the Newman Club on campus and throughout Middle Atlantic Province that included the states of Pennsylvania, Maryland, Delaware, and the District of Columbia. Concluding his senior year at Penn State, Robert was elected the 1st Vice President of the National Newman Club Federation. While working with the Newman Club, Robert would meet his future wife, Jeanne Claire Fritz who was Miss Clarion State Teachers College and a graduate librarian of that institution. The couple would marry on Thanksgiving Day in 1958 and have three sons over the next ten years.

Robert would be employed in the Catholic school system in St. Marys, Pennsylvania for seven years before moving to the public school system in Johnsonburg, Pennsylvania, a community ten miles from St. Marys. During the summers, Robert worked on improving his education. When retiring in 1992, he had a Master Degree from Wesleyan University in Connecticut and did a year of graduate course work at Penn State in Horticulture. During the same time period, he acquired a CDL license with all endorsements, an auctioneer's license, and all the licenses that one can receive in the field of cosmetology. He also established the Academy of Beauty Culture, Inc. in St. Marys that he sold upon retirement.

In 1996 he transitioned, and on June 8, 1999 became Roberta Lynn Dostal. She attended Lancaster Theological Seminary and graduated with a Masters Degree in Religious Education. She presently resides in Johnstown, Pennsylvania. Roberta returned to Johnstown to care for her aging mother who passed away in 2004 at the age of 101. The past ten years, Roberta has been active in attending course work at the University of Pittsburgh at Johnstown. Roberta is extremely thankful to the university for the opportunity to continue her education at age 80. Ms. Dostal is a member of the Main Line Unitarian Church in Devon, Pennsylvania and crosses the state about twice a month to worship in her church and visit with friends she made while living there before returning to Johnstown.

Made in the USA
Charleston, SC
30 November 2015